MEETING
✿ OTHER
BELIEVERS

CARDINAL FRANCIS ARINZE

The Risks
and Rewards
of Interreligious
Dialogue

MEETING
OTHER
BELIEVERS

Our Sunday Visitor Publishing Division
Our Sunday Visitor, Inc.
Huntington, Indiana 46750

First published in 1997 by Gracewing, Fowler Wright Books, © 1997 by Francis Cardinal Arinze. This edition published by Our Sunday Visitor, Inc., by special arrangement with the original publisher. If any copyrighted materials have been inadvertently used in this work without proper credit being given in one manner or another, please notify Our Sunday Visitor in writing so that future printings of this work may be corrected accordingly.

Our Sunday Visitor Publishing Division
Our Sunday Visitor, Inc.
200 Noll Plaza
Huntington, Indiana 46750

International Standard Book Number: 0-87973-949-5
Library of Congress Catalog Card Number: 98-65358

Cover design by Monica Watts

PRINTED IN THE UNITED STATES OF AMERICA

949

Contents

Preface to the U.S. Edition

IT IS ENCOURAGING THAT *MEETING OTHER BELIEVERS* IS BEING given a U.S. edition.

While Christians are the majority among the citizens and residents of the U.S.A., there is an impressive presence of other believers: Jews, Muslims, Buddhists, Hindus, Sikhs, Jains, and people of original North American religions. Religious plurality is definitely a fact in the United States.

There is a considerable effort being made in this large country to promote good understanding, harmony, and cooperation across religious frontiers. The United States Catholic Bishops' Conference has in Washington, D.C., an office for Interreligious Affairs, which is dynamic in its contacts with other believers. Many dioceses across the country take various initiatives in this field. There is a long tradition of contacts between Christians and Jews, but in recent years relations with Muslims have also been growing. Buddhists and Christians are meeting too. Worthy of special mention is the symposium in Gethsemani Trappist Abbey in summer 1996 between Catholic monks and nuns and their Buddhist counterparts. The meeting of many world religions in Chicago in 1993, as a celebration of the centenary of the first "Parliament of World Religions," increased attention to the need for contacts across religious dividing lines. It has led some to ask if some more concrete forms of collaboration may not be needed.

My hope therefore is that these personal reflections, *Meeting Other Believers,* may be found useful in the context of the various interreligious initiatives of today and tomorrow in the U.S. The book makes an effort to give an answer to people's doubts, fears, and questions as they encounter people of differing religious persuasions. It seeks to encourage these contacts and to suggest ways to reduce the risks to a minimum and maximize the potential for good of such encounters.

If both the veteran practitioners of interreligious dialogue and the hesitant beginners find these reflections of some use, the effort made in putting them together will have been worthwhile.

CARDINAL FRANCIS ARINZE
Rome
November 1997

Introduction

IN OUR TIMES, PEOPLE OF DIFFERENT RELIGIONS ARE MEETING AND interacting more perhaps than in any other period of human history. Relations across religious frontiers are not just being discussed. They are taking place. And they are increasing.

I have noticed growing interest in interreligious dialogue among a rather wide range of people. Statesmen and ambassadors have shown appreciation for the religious dimension in human affairs and for the need of cordial relations between people of different religions for the good of society. Busy bishops, hardworking parish priests, and dedicated theologians have asked themselves what the place of interreligious dialogue should be in their overall ministry. I have met both Christian and Buddhist monks really interested in how they can go beyond courtesy, show better understanding and appreciation, and establish some cooperation with people of another religion who are dedicated to spiritual engagements and pursuits analogous to theirs. Academicians, doctors, lawyers, teachers, and other professionals are asking themselves why they should become involved in interreligious relations. There are members of religious movements or associations, Christian and otherwise, and also university students, seminarians, and aspirants to consecrated religious life, who want to make a more committed engagement to interaction with people of other religions.

One must not forget those religious leaders who are themselves convinced of the importance of interreligious dialogue, but who have quite a problem trying to convince some of their coreligionists of this necessity in the world of today.

There are some enthusiasts for interreligious relations who do not seem to have a wide-enough picture of the different elements and of the considerations that should be taken into account. Incurable optimists as they are, they see interreligious dialogue as the solution to most problems of society today, or as the soul of true religion, and they do not give enough weight to the difficulties that are by no means imaginary.

At the other extreme are the doubters and head-shakers. They are not convinced that interreligious dialogue will do much good. Indeed, they fear that it may cause an erosion of genuine faith or lead to syncretism, to a religion of nobody that does no good to anybody. They may have seen or heard of real abuses of interreligious dialogue. Under pressure, they are ready to accept it as an academic exercise. But they regard such an exercise as rather sterile and they think that the time dedicated to it could have been put to better use.

Some experiences that I have had since 1984, when the Holy Father, Pope John Paul II, called me to the Pontifical Council for Interreligious Dialogue, seem to me to suggest answers to the above-mentioned desires, questions, doubts, and engagements. I have had many opportunities to visit, and to be visited by, qualified representatives of other religions, to listen to them, to ask them questions, and generally to interact with them. Visits to their places of worship have been instructive. Opportunities to observe the works of art, projects of social service, and sheer spiritual discipline and asceticism inspired by their religions have been to me a help to meditation and prayer.

One must also not forget the ability of religion, seriously believed in and generously practiced, to promote a meeting of hearts, the fashioning of true friendship across religious borders. Often hearts meet before heads. When we love a person, we are better positioned to understand that person and to experience greater appreciation of whatever that person has that is true, noble, good, beautiful, or holy.

It seems to me a pity not to share such experiences in writing with a wider public. Some friends have suggested to me to move along the road that this little book represents.

There are hardworking individuals and members of interreligious dialogue groups or associations who have shared their experiences with me and who might welcome a written feedback. They may see the following pages not only as an echo of their experiences, but also as an overall personal reflection that can be regarded as a tribute to the pioneers of dialogue and a help to beginners in the enterprise.

Some Christians will welcome an exposition of the theological reasons that underpin the engagement of the Church in the apostolate of interreligious dialogue. How does this ministry fit into the general mandate that the Church received from her Divine Founder?

From the above lines, the reader will draw the conclusion that the following pages are meant to be a record of personal experiences and reflections. Almost like a long conversation, they will try to spell out my convictions on interreligious dialogue, the necessity of this engagement as I see it, some problems and challenges, some hoped-for benefits, and the ideal climate in which dialogue prospers. The possible risks will not be glossed over. But the way to avoid them and to get the best out of this necessity of our times will also be surveyed.

This is therefore not going to be a work of scholarly research, a thesis studded with quotations. It is going to be a simple and straightforward sharing of experiences and convictions. My hope and prayer is that the reader may find in it a help and a suggestion to better promote walking together and working together with other believers.

CARDINAL FRANCIS ARINZE
Vatican City
November 24, 1996

cHАPТЕr
1 ·

The Essence of

Interreligious Dialogue

IT IS IMPORTANT AT THE OUTSET TO DEFINE THE PARAMETERS OF what we are discussing. Briefly, interreligious dialogue can be defined and described as follows.

What It Is Not

Interreligious dialogue is not the same as the study of the various religions and a comparison of them, although such a discipline is important and useful.

Debate between followers of various religions, no matter how friendly, is not interreligious dialogue. In dialogue encounters, one is not trying to prove oneself right and the other believer wrong.

Interreligious dialogue is not the same as ecumenism. Ecumenism refers to all initiatives — prayers, meetings, dialogues, common projects, etc. — to promote the reunion of Christians in one Church according to the will of Christ, the Founder. Ecumenism is therefore only between Christian religious communities or churches. Interreligious dialogue, on the other hand, refers to relations between Christians and other believers such as Jews, Muslims, Hindus, Buddhists, and followers of Traditional Religions. It does not aim at bringing about the unity of all religions in a kind of super-religion.

Interreligious dialogue is not an effort to persuade the other person to embrace one's own religion, although we cannot deny to any believer the right to wish to share one's religion with another. Effort at such conversion should be clearly distinguished from interreligious dialogue, as will be done in greater detail in a later chapter.

What It Is

Interreligious dialogue is a meeting of people of differing religions, in an atmosphere of freedom and openness, in order to listen to the other, to try to understand that person's religion, and hopefully to seek possibilities of collaboration. It is hoped that the other partner will reciprocate, because dialogue should be marked by a two-way and not a one-way movement. Reciprocity is in the nature of dialogue. There is give and take. Dialogue implies both receptivity and active communication.

I mentioned listening as one of the first acts of dialogue. It is important to stress this, because more and more people are finding it difficult to listen to others. Willingness to listen implies appreciation of what the other person is, believes, prays, or lives, together with a conviction that it is worthwhile sacrificing some time to be informed about all that. The person who is very willing to talk but not so prepared to listen is not likely to be a good dialogue partner. Sometimes the most direct road to a person's heart and trust is simply the willingness to listen, to ask questions for clarification, and to seek to understand.

Various Forms of Dialogue

Interreligious dialogue can take many different forms. Four major types of dialogue have been identified by dialogue experts without any suggestion that one form is necessarily superior to another.

There is first what has come to be called *dialogue of life*. It is the form of interreligious dialogue most within the reach of anyone who lives or interacts with believers in a different religion. Dialogue of life is interreligious relationship at the level of the ordinary relational situations of daily life: family, school, place of social or cultural contact, village meetings, workplace, politics, trade, or commerce. When neighbors of differing religions are open to one another, when they share their projects and hopes, concerns and sorrows, they are engaging in dialogue of life. They do not necessarily discuss religion. But they draw on the values of their different beliefs and traditions. Without giving it this name, this is what Charles de Foucauld (1858-1916) was doing for years, when out of love for the people of Tamanrasset, who are Muslims, he lived among them as one of them. Many of the Little Sisters and Little Brothers of Jesus, who share his spirit, still do the same among Muslim populations. I visited nine Carmelite nuns who located their monastery in Marawi City, Philippines, in an almost totally Muslim town, to show their love for the Muslims.

A second type of interreligious dialogue is the *dialogue of action*. This refers to Christians and other believers cooperating for the promotion of human development and liberation in all its forms. Joint projects for human advancement can take the form, as I saw in one country, of a Muslim group and a Catholic group forming a committee to run a leprosy-control clinic and center. In another country, women from two religions joined hands to rescue street women and help them find acceptable employment. I know a Buddhist organization that has cooperated with a Catholic one to help in an area ravaged by drought, famine, and poverty. In April 1991 a meeting was held in Malta to seek to establish practical cooperation on the global humanitarian problem of refugees and migrants. The meeting was an initiative of three Christian organizations (the International Catholic Migration Commission, the Lutheran World Federation, and the World Council of Churches) and three Islamic organizations (the World Islamic Call Society, the World Muslim Congress, and the World Islamic Call Foundation). Among its declarations, we read: "We affirm that we must work together to ensure that the rights and dignity of all peoples on the move, and their families if separated, are respected and upheld no matter who these people are or wherever they may be found."

When we talk of the *dialogue of discourse*, we think of experts in Christianity and other religions meeting to exchange information on their respective religious beliefs and heritages. They listen to one another in an effort to understand the religion of the others at a deep level, and as articulated by qualified and well-prepared representatives of the other religious traditions. They try to see what beliefs and practices they share and where they differ. Together they try to face modern problems and challenges in the light of their differing religions. This type of dialogue, of its nature, is for specialists. An example of such dialogue is that promoted by the Groupe de Recherches Islamo-Chrétien (GRIC), which was founded in 1977 and which assembles committed Christians and Muslims that do theological study together. The GRIC has produced three publications: *Ces Écritures qui nous questionnent* (or *The Challenge of the Scriptures*), on the Bible and the Qur'an, *Foi et Justice*, and *Pluralisme et Laicité* (neither of which have as yet been translated). There is also the group called al-Líqâ, or Encounter, among Palestinians.

A fourth form of interreligious dialogue is the *dialogue of religious experience*. It refers to persons deeply rooted in their own religious traditions sharing experiences of meditation, prayer, contemplation, faith and its expression, ways of searching for God as the Absolute or of living the monastic or eremitic life, and also mysticism. This form of exchange is indicated for persons who are committed to a more than ordinary pursuit of spiritual progress. There are *de facto* Catholic Benedictine and Trappist monks who have carefully planned inter-monastic exchanges with Buddhist counterparts. Such communications generally include several weeks' stay in the monastery of the other in silence and in the sharing of what is possible and advisable.

It is clear that the above forms of dialogue do not exclude one another, that no one is expected to practice all forms in all circumstances, but that whenever a believer meets another of a different religious conviction, at least one form of dialogue is possible.

cHAPTER
2

Interreligious Dialogue
Is Not Optional

IT IS NOW IMPERATIVE TO FACE DIRECTLY THE QUESTION: IS INTER-religious dialogue really necessary? Granted that it is a suitable pursuit for university eggheads and ivory-tower theologians, but can a busy religious leader, bishop, priest, lawyer, doctor, or industrialist really afford the time for it? How is the ordinary citizen in the crowded city, or the poor village farmer, to be convinced of the urgency of interreligious dialogue?

The following considerations are offered as an answer.

Religious Plurality

Religious plurality is a fact. In the world of today this reality is being more increasingly brought to our notice. Christians form about 33 percent of the total world population. Of that figure, Catholics count for 18 percent and other Christians 15 percent. Muslims number 17 percent, Hindus 13 percent, Buddhists 7 percent, and Jews 0.5 percent. But there are also Traditional Re-

ligionists, Sikhs, Jainists, Zoroastrians, Baha'is, Shintoists, and others (cf. David Barrett: *World Christian
Encyclopaedia*, Nairobi, 1982, p. 6).

These religions are the ways of life of a greater part
of humanity. They are the living expressions of the souls
of vast groups of people. They carry with them the echo
of thousands of years of humanity looking for God. And
no matter what mistakes humanity may have made (and
religious truth is not always easy to arrive at, and is even
more difficult to live for long without special help from
God), we cannot doubt the sincerity of heart and the
moral and spiritual stature of many religious leaders
along the corridors of history. Moreover, the world's religions possess an impressive patrimony of deeply religious texts and of the assimilated wisdom of peoples and
cultures. They have taught generations of people how
to pray, how to live, how to die, and how to look after
their deceased ones (cf. Paul VI: *Evangelii Nuntiandi*,
53).

It would be most unrealistic to ignore all this and
live as if there were only one religion in the world.

Desire for Interaction

In the world of our times, people of differing religions meet much more frequently than in past centuries. Opportunities for travel and for instant communications worldwide are now greater than in any other
period of human history. People from Asia visit Europe

and America or settle down to live in these continents in bigger numbers than ever before. Europeans and Americans go to Asia. The wide-bodied intercontinental jets are not lacking in passengers. Africa and Europe know each other more than they ever did before. Oceania is not left out. The sciences of anthropology, ethnology, and religions have made tremendous progress. The term "global village," as applied to a world in which communications are shortening distances, is not altogether an exaggeration.

It is not just the desire for travel that brings about this encounter, but also more serious circumstances. The upheavals brought about by famine or other natural disasters, by wars or internal conflicts, have displaced large numbers of people. Economic necessity also drives people to seek employment elsewhere. All this has added to increased contact between people of different religious traditions.

It is not only that peoples are meeting one another, bringing with them their cultures and religions. It is also that they want to meet. Isolationism is being frowned upon more and more. What people and religions have in common is being increasingly recognized as more important than what divides them. Religious believers want to be well informed about other religions whose adherents are now their neighbors or colleagues. They are no longer satisfied with labels and generalized judgments earlier passed on the entire religious family of the other. In short, they want interreligious relations.

Mutual Enrichment

Interreligious dialogue can help each participant to grow in his or her own faith when that partner in dialogue encounters a person of another religious persuasion and engages in sincere and calm confrontation of religious beliefs, practices, and values. Sometimes a religious conviction is better appreciated, further studied and deepened, understood and lived with greater commitment, when met with other views. Another religious believer can also challenge us in the best sense of the word. When, for example, I visited Buddhist monasteries in Thailand and I learned that the monks sleep on hard beds, eat only once a day, avoid meat and fish, and have the vow of celibacy, I was implicitly challenged to live with greater commitment the riches of Christian asceticism. When I notice that a sincere Muslim prays at stated times five times a day, and that he does not allow human respect to prevent him from doing this at a railway station, or by coming away from a colloquium or social gathering, then I cannot avoid asking myself why some Christians are hesitant to make the Sign of the Cross in a restaurant, or to pray their Rosary in a bus, or to recite the Angelus in some other public place.

There is no doubt that a participant in interreligious dialogue, while remaining firmly rooted in his or her religion, can grow spiritually through interreligious encounters, on condition that the person remains open to the action of God, which can come through the dialogue partner.

Interaction and Mutual Enrichment of Religions

It is not only individual participants who can be enriched through interreligious contacts. It is also their religions themselves.

Through interreligious contacts, for example, Christianity can contribute to other religions' elevation, inspiration, and universality. Christianity has helped some religions to shed some of their unworthy beliefs and practices such as human sacrifice, the killing of twins, or the denial of some human rights to unborn children or to women. It has helped Buddhism to show more interest in social work and initiatives toward human promotion. A Buddhist nun who promotes many social services in Taiwan told me that she learned this dimension of religion from Catholic Ursuline Sisters. Buddhists and Muslims can see in Christianity a religion that gives women a higher status than theirs. Traditional Religions can see in Christianity a fulfillment of many of their not fully articulated longings for contact with God, the Supreme Spirit.

There is also the question of the relationship between religion, country, and culture. In some majority

Buddhist or Islamic countries, there is the danger of identifying the country's culture with Buddhism or Islam. Examples are Thailand and some Arab countries. Some Hindus think that to be Indian is to be Hindu. Christians, especially Catholics, bring to dialogue a universalism that is remarkable. The Church has unity in doctrine and in religious authority, but at the same time a firm belief in the right of the human person to religious freedom. And the Church makes a serious effort to respect people's cultures, languages, ways of worship, and national character in the same family of faith. Indeed Christianity is really saying: God is our Father, and we are all brothers and sisters; let us hold hands together, let us work together, and make the world a better place in which to live. This message is welcomed by many religions of the world. The desire of other believers to meet the Pope, to come to Rome, and to work with Catholics, even when they do not accept some major elements of Catholic faith and morals, is a sign of this appreciation and desire for an exchange of gifts.

Christianity also receives from the other religions when they meet. These religions bring along with them the cultural patterns in which they flourish: languages, philosophical categories, ritual expressions, and local styles proper to their peoples. They can enrich the expression and practice of Christianity with these gifts. In this sense, interreligious dialogue can help to promote what has come to be known as inculturation in theological circles: the incarnation of Christianity among different peoples and cultures. The Second Vatican Council wisely noted that the Church fosters and takes to herself "in so far as they are good, the ability, resources and customs of each people. Taking them to herself, she purifies, strengthens and ennobles them. The Church in this is mindful that she must harvest with the King to Whom the nations were given for an inheritance and into whose city they bring gifts and presents" (*Lumen Gentium*, 13). The Church is aware of her call to universality and appreciates the fact that contact with other religions can help her to express this.

Harmony Between Citizens

If citizens of the same country or region belong to different religions, they can find in interreligious dialogue a help to build up and strengthen harmony in society. Acceptance of others, with all that differentiates them from one's own religious community, is very much a requirement of harmony. The alternative is to ignore one another, to label others with unacceptable generalizations, or, worse still, to engage in rivalry, to foster tension, or to wade into violence.

Religion in itself is not the cause of factions, violence, and war. Every religion worthy of the name teaches the Golden Rule: to treat others as one would like to be treated. However, when religion is abused in order to motivate people to engage in violence, the results can indeed be negative. This can happen when the real motives of the promoters are economic, racial, political, or desires of revenge, or pure jealousy. This shows why religious leaders have the duty to show their coreligionists the genuine face of religion and to convince them that it is a contradiction of true religion to engage in violence. To kill others in the name of God or religion is a travesty of what genuine religion is all about.

Community leaders, statesmen, political figures, and all citizens need to be convinced that the abuse or hijacking of religion in order to foment enmities and violence can wound and cripple a community or country. Pope John Paul II drew attention to the contribution of interreligious relations to promote harmony when he spoke to distinguished representatives of many world religions gathered at the Assisi World Day of Prayer for Peace on October 27, 1986: "Either we learn to walk together in peace and harmony, or we drift apart and ruin ourselves and others. We hope that this pilgrimage to Assisi has taught us anew to be aware of the common origin and common destiny of humanity. Let us see in it an anticipation of what God would like the developing history of humanity to be: a fraternal journey in which we accompany one another towards the transcendent goal which He sets for us" (John Paul II: Concluding Address at Assisi, 5, in *Assisi, World Day of Prayer for Peace*; Rome: Pontifical Commission "Justitia et Pax," 1987, pp. 95-96).

Joint Promotion of Moral Values, Development, Justice, and Peace

When the followers of the various religions in a country or region not only live in harmony but also positively cooperate, then they can do much to promote moral values, development in all its forms, and more justice in society. They thus prepare the way for peace.

While a few people are enough to cause tension, confusion, and destruction, the cooperation of all is needed in order to promote lasting development, justice, and peace. There are problems and challenges that do not respect religious frontiers: corruption in public life, wrong attitude to work or to the good of the country, and discrimination against people because of their color, ethnic background, or sex. There are development questions that no one religious community can solve single-handedly: uncontrolled urbanization, the growing gap between the rich and the poor, runaway inflation.

All these and similar challenges are best faced when all believers, drawing from the highest ideals of their respective religions, work together to find adequate solutions. After all, there is no separate Catholic drought, or Jewish epidemic, or Muslim urbanization, or Buddhist inflation, or Sikh poverty, or Hindu embezzlement of public funds. All these are problems and challenges of the whole society. Interreligious effort to face them is not optional. It is obligatory. Such collaboration is even more urgent when the problems are due to the human will: oppression of the poor, tribalism, religious discrimination, and erosion of sound family values.

May I give two examples of interreligious collaboration in such matters? The World Conference on Religion and Peace is a multireligious organization founded by Christians, Muslims, Buddhists, Hindus, and others to help remove discriminations and to promote justice and peace. It has its headquarters in New York. It has helped to rally believers in concrete action within a number of countries and on the international level. It held its first world assembly in Kyoto in 1970.

A second example refers to cooperation between Catholics and Muslims during the United Nations' Conference on Population and Development in Cairo in September 1994. Three sections of the preparatory document that could not leave a genuine Catholic and a true Muslim indifferent were those that suggested the acceptance of abortion and homosexuality and tacit approval of a free exercise of sexual activity among youth as a condition for the poorer countries to receive financial assistance. The Holy See delegation and the delegations from many majority Muslim countries, sharing a common opposition to these evils, joined hands to try to get those sections of the document changed. Of course, this did not mean that all differences between Muslims and Catholics had vanished. But at least they were able to join hands to defend some real family values.

Solutions to Religious Extremism

More than one country is troubled by religious extremists. These are people who, in their desire to be faithful to what they consider to be the original and undiluted form of their religion, adopt extreme measures toward other believers, or even toward the more moderate members of their own religious community. They, for example, want all religions to be illegal in their country except their own religion, and to promote this they are ready even to kill. They sometimes insist on a particular article of clothing, for example, for women, and will use violence against those who do not comply. In one country they even made out a list of words that adherents of other religions are not allowed to use.

Many of the major religions in the world have, or have had, religious extremists. Some are more violent than others. All of them are intolerant. The religious extremists, or fundamentalists as some call them, may be sincere and in good faith. But at the same time they are trampling on the rights of others. They are violating the principle of religious freedom, which says that no one is to use force on another human being in matters of conscience, in matters religious. Religion should well up from the human soul as a free offering to God, as a free response of the human creature to God the Creator.

All genuine religious leaders, as well as thoughtful civil authorities, are worried by the phenomenon of religious extremism. Interreligious relations can, and should, help to moderate the "zeal" of the extremists, to convince them to accommodate others, beginning with the more moderate members of their own religion, and to lead them to forge their swords into farm instruments, to build up and not to pull down.

Unity of Human Nature

The final reason that I shall propose for the necessity of interreligious relations is the unity of human nature. It is the one God who created every man and woman. Human nature is shared equally by all. Each human being is essentially body and soul, matter and spirit, a being gifted with intelligence and will. More important still, every human being has a desire, hidden or open, for a transcendent God. And everyone notices his or her inability to reach Him if totally unaided.

In the various religions, people are seeking answers to the fundamental questions that have tormented human existence in all ages. Among them are questions about human origin and destiny, the essence of happiness, the meaning of evil and sin, the reason for suffering, and, especially, that Being who explains all other beings.

Some of the religions have put together what the human soul looking for God and for answers to the above questions has been able to arrive at. Some religions believe that they have received explicit revelations from God in one form or another.

It is true that there are wide differences between the religions. But it is also true that there are convergences or at least analogies. If for no other reasons, then at least because of the unity of human nature, the followers of the religions of the world should meet, listen to one another, try to understand one another, and see what they can do together. That is what interreligious dialogue is all about.

CHAPTER 3

The Risks of
Interreligious Dialogue

WHAT SHALL WE REPLY TO A PERSON WHO ARGUES THUS: "I ACCEPT all that has been said in the preceding chapter. I see the point that interreligious dialogue is not optional in the world of today. But I consider it dangerous. I have seen it do harm to some of my coreligionists. It is risky. Danger of losing one's faith, relativism, syncretism, and religious indifferentism are some of the risks."

As an answer let me begin by admitting that I share most of these concerns. The way to a solution seems to me to be found among the following considerations.

Danger of Losing One's Faith

Some people fear that in interreligious dialogue they may meet other believers who are theologically better prepared than themselves, more sophisticated, and better able to articulate their religious beliefs and practices. Or the religion of the other person may be better structured institutionally and armed with more personnel, centers for higher religious studies, and hard cash.

Some fear a religion they regard as politically powerful. The overall risk, the argument goes, is that the "weaker" partner in dialogue may become confused, may be theologically overpowered, and may be imperceptibly wheeled into religious doubt, or into abandoning his or her religion and embracing that of the more "powerful" dialogue partner.

The answer is that interreligious dialogue need not take the form of theological discussion at all. It may just be what was called *dialogue of life* above, or cooperation in social projects. Moreover, even when it is a question of theological dialogue, it is not advisable for a believer who is theologically unprepared to meet a theology professor from another religion. A certain parity of cultural and educational background is required for fair and fruitful theological exchange.

In all cases, whether for the learned or for the less articulate, it is most important that one should be sincerely convinced of one's own faith and deeply grounded in it before one can fruitfully and without undue risk meet people of a different religious conviction.

Risk of Relativism

Others fear that to meet other believers often can cause such erosion in one's religious tenets that finally a person ends up believing that one religion is as good as another. This is the error of religious relativism, the mistake of those who say that all religions are roads to the same God, and that it does not matter to what religion a person chooses to belong, as long as the person has good will.

Let us distinguish between sincerity and objectivity. Sincerity is very important especially in religious matters, because good will, good conscience, honesty, lack of deceit, and freedom from duplicity are fundamental religious requirements. But objectivity is no less important, since everyone is bound to look for the objective religious truth and, having found it, the person is bound to embrace it. And every person will have to answer before God for all religious choices. This is one of the reasons for the principle of religious liberty.

To the error of religious relativism we therefore reply that one religion is not as good as another, that the religions are not all saying the same thing on every point at issue, and that every individual has personal responsibility, and therefore freedom, to look for objective religious truth. This clear mind about the existence of objective truth, allied with respect for everyone's religion even when one disagrees with some aspects of it, is a necessary requirement for safe and fruitful interreligious dialogue.

Fear of Syncretism

An allied fear to relativism is that of syncretism. Syncretism is the effort to put several religions together and to carve a new religion out of them. The effort may be guided by the desire to preserve all the factors that seem common to all the religions, a type of religious highest common denominator. It may be the desire not to offend any of the believers but rather to work out a pattern in which none of them feels threatened.

It is not often that people would propose syncretism in theory as a new religion. Nevertheless, some have *de facto* engaged in syncretism by pulling, for example, some Christian beliefs into African Traditional Religion within Africa or in Latin America or vice versa. Others have coined "new religions" in Europe by mixing up elements of Hinduism and Buddhism with Christianity and ancient pre-Christian religions.

Syncretism may more often appear in particular practices such as interreligious prayer, when it does not respect the religious identity of the participants but presents them as members of one religious community of faith. There can also be examples of ritual, religious dress, religious titles, or building styles over which even believers in one religion can disagree whether there is really syncretism, or whether they are only instances of adaptation, or inculturation, or indigenization of one or other religion.

Syncretism is a danger that has to be watched in interreligious relations. No attempt should be made to nibble at the religious identity of any of the participants.

At the same time, the necessity of a religion that lays claim to universality to seek to be at home among all peoples and cultures cannot be denied. The Catholic Church, for example, believes that it is in her very nature to be at home in every culture. Not even the fear of possible syncretism will discourage her from efforts at inculturation. Theologians and pastors should rather exercise their office of clarification, guidance, and vigilance.

Fear of the Flock Seeking Pastures Elsewhere

Some religious leaders are hesitant to encourage their coreligionists to make friends with people of other religions because they fear that their flock may seek more satisfying pastures elsewhere. Some bishops and priests in Europe, for example, are noticing that some of their Christians, especially from among the young, are falling in love with some elements of Hinduism, Buddhism, Shintoism, or some other Oriental religions. They are fascinated by Oriental methods of meditation. They are sitting at the feet of Japanese *roshis* and Indian *gurus*. They are practicing *yoga* and *Zen*. Some of them are flying to Asian countries to make direct contact with these religions at their source. I have personally met U.S. Christians who have become Buddhist monks and nuns in Thailand and in Taiwan.

The risk is real. But it applies rather to the type of Christian who is not well grounded in the Christian faith and practice. Unfortunately there are many, especially among the young, who are abysmally ignorant of the major tenets of Christianity. They do not know about the riches of Christian asceticism or mysticism. For them, St. Teresa of Ávila, St. John of the Cross, St. Catherine of Siena, St. Francis of Assisi, and St. Theresa of the Holy Child Jesus are mere names whose spiritualities are largely a closed book to them.

Christian pastors who have such religiously rootless Christians have to ask themselves to what extent they have helped their coreligionists to make progress in personal or mental prayer. Have the youth found in their pastors spiritual masters at the feet of whom they have learned how to pray, and not just how to read prayers already printed out, no matter the irreplaceable necessity of fixed liturgical prayer? Moreover, Catholic monasteries can ask themselves whether the surrounding Catholic community sees in them centers of silence in searching for the face of God, sacred places for initiation into contemplation or prayer of the heart, and seedbeds of mysticism. And Christian families can ask themselves how much religious instruction, family prayer, and family reception of the sacraments are to be found in their homes.

If young Christians are maimed by religious ignorance of the riches of Christian life and mysticism, and are tormented by spiritual hunger for some elevating spiritual practices, is it any wonder if they go spiritual shopping among Oriental religions, or even among the sects, new religious movements, or esoteric groups? This is the explanation that an experienced French priest gave me when I asked him why some Catholic young people flirt with other religions. And I think he has a point.

Danger of Religious Indifferentism

There is also the fear that frequent contact with people of other religious convictions may lead some believers to lose belief in any one religion. They may begin by putting some beliefs of their religion in parentheses, by suspending their belief in some tenets for some time. This is already a sign that there is a problem. But they may move on to a general doubt about their own religion and then about every other religion. Some of such religious indifferentists try to justify their position by presenting themselves as liberal, or as broad-minded as opposed to fanatical, or simply as post-Christian!

Such a position is erroneous because there is such a thing as objective religious truth not based on people's opinions. Every teacher knows that sincerity is not the only virtue required of the student. Knowledge of the objective truth and ability to state it are also necessary.

Religious indifferentism can be avoided in interreligious contacts if the participants are well grounded in their own religions, if they live these religions with sincerity and authenticity, if they are well adjusted to their faith community, and if their religious community takes an interest in their interreligious contacts.

As the reader can see, there are real risks involved

in interreligious dialogue. But they are not unavoidable. The worst fears need not be realized. And the best results can be obtained, if only the necessary steps are taken. Everyone who rides a bicycle or drives a car understands this. The adequate answer to possible risks is not to renounce the whole exercise but to ride or drive carefully!

cHAPTEr
4

Religious Identity
and Dialogue

OUR REFLECTION MUST NOW TAKE ANOTHER STEP FORWARD. IT should now focus on the place of one's religious identity in interreligious dialogue. The question can be thus stated: Granted that interreligious dialogue is necessary and that the possible risks in its exercise can be avoided, there still remains the question of how much one's religious distinctiveness should show itself in interreligious contacts. Is care not needed to avoid provoking others? Is it not more prudent to go easy on what distinguishes one from other believers and just to dwell on what all can share? This seemingly simple request needs closer examination.

Dialogue Presumes Differences

If all humanity were members of only one religion, if all held the same beliefs, worshiped in the same way, and had the same code of conduct, there would be no need for interreligious dialogue. Dialogue presumes that there is diversity in religion.

It follows that a partner in such dialogue is authentic when that person is a good representative of his or her religious community. Then the other believers are clear about whom they are meeting. There can be an exchange of gifts because none of the participants is a photocopy of the other. A Catholic priest recently told me that he regularly meets other believers. On one occasion, a fellow Catholic priest, in the presence of the other believers, remarked that this priest was rather conservative, always wore a Roman collar, and always repeated the Pope's teachings. But a person of another religious persuasion intervened to say that she preferred to meet the Father as he was, because then she knew the correct Catholic position. In short, she was saying that she was happy that the priest kept his Catholic identity.

Christians who, while engaged in interreligious relations, would like to hide their Christian identity, or at least to de-emphasize it, seem to be saying, without words, that Christ is an obstacle or an embarrassment to dialogue, and that they have found a better formula for contact with others that consists in setting aside for the moment that they are sent by Christ. To state the situation in these terms is to show that an authentic Christian should not adopt such a stance. As Christians, we should realize and recognize who we are and to Whom we are witnesses. Only then can we be good ambassadors of the Christian faith community. And if we are Catholics, we should not hide this when we meet others. We do not promote dialogue authentically by suppressing our religious identity.

If, therefore, a dialogue partner loses his or her religious identity, then there is now no one left with whom to hold a dialogue. If the partner is hiding his or her identity, there can be several kinds of misgivings, like suspicion, mistaken identity, belief that there is agreement where in fact there is none, and so on. And if the partner is confused about his or her religious image, or is in search of a seemingly lost religious identity card, the consequences are not any less unpleasant.

It should therefore be accepted that a clear picture to oneself of what one is with reference to religious affiliation, together with a quiet and sincere presentation of one's religious "visiting card," are among the fundamental requirements for fruitful interreligious dialogue. Such identity can refer to beliefs held, rites of prayer or worship, moral law or code of conduct, religious dress, or even religious terminology. Let us take some examples.

<u>Religious Identity in Statement of Belief</u>

Interreligious relations are not religious negotiation conferences where the representatives of each religion strive to see how many of their beliefs they can sell to others by expert bargaining. Interreligious dialogue is not even primarily or necessarily a statement and discussion of beliefs.

We must, however, grant that a group of theologically well-prepared representatives of several religions can meet so often that mutual trust has grown up between them, and that they are now well able to listen to one another's statements of beliefs, with all their convergences and divergences. If a group has reached that level of mutual confidence, the participants should not be silent on points of belief where the group differs.

Accordingly, a Catholic who is meeting a Muslim should not soft-pedal beliefs in the Most Blessed Trinity (three Persons in only one God), in Jesus Christ as Son of God and God, in the Son of God becoming man and dying on the Cross for the salvation of all humanity, and in the Most Blessed Virgin Mary as the Mother of God. Muslims do not accept these doctrines. But a sincere, friendly Muslim dialogue partner should not get angry that Catholics hold them. On the other hand, a Muslim in dialogue should not hesitate to state that Muslims hold that the Qur'an is the last revelation from God and Muhammad the greatest and the last of the prophets.

Buddhists do not speak about God or the soul, but Christians would be unauthentic if they did not. Sincerity about one's religious beliefs is part of dialogue.

The use of terms that have acquired definite meanings within religious communities needs particular attention when believers in different religions meet. Words like God, Divine Person, soul, heaven, salvation, redemption, perfection, grace, merit, charity, sin, and hell do not necessarily mean the same things to Christians, Muslims, Buddhists, Hindus, and African Traditional Religionists. If such words are used in interreligious encounters, care should be taken to make their meaning clear. And a believer should not be too quick to copy a word loaded with meaning from another religion because of the dangers of misunderstanding and sometimes of unintended offense.

Religious Identity in Worship

Most of the major religions of the world have a formally laid-out rite for public worship or prayer. They differ in the degree of detail or regulation. An authentic believer will worship according to the officially approved way of his or her religious family.

In the Catholic Church, which I know best, there is, for example, a clear distinction between public prayer in the name of the Church (also called liturgical prayer), community prayer said by a group in their own name, and personal prayer particular to an individual. The Catholic Church is rather detailed in what she lays down for public prayer. Even the words and readings are fixed. There are some sections where the initiative of the chief celebrant or of the assembly is allowed in the introduction of their own words.

It would therefore be a mistake for a Catholic priest to make changes that violate Church regulations and practice when he is celebrating the Holy Eucharist, just because some of the people present at that celebration come from other religions and will not agree with some of the formulas read out of Church books. Similarly, it would be wrong at a Catholic Eucharistic celebration to bring in readings from the sacred books of other religions, even if the ideas expressed in these are acceptable to Catholics. The reason is that authenticity, sincerity, and clear religious identity are expected of a dialogue partner, and sound Catholic practice does not allow such readings at Mass. Moreover, a reasonable Buddhist, Muslim, or Jew who attends a Eucharistic celebration in the Catholic Church is not expecting an interreligiously agreed rite, but should find it normal to see how his or her Catholic friends celebrate their public worship.

Religious Identity in Comportment

Most religions have prescriptions on how their followers are to behave in private or public life. The Catholic Church, for example, has a rather developed concept on how to live the faith as a follower of Christ. A branch of her theology deals with right and wrong in matters of human conduct. She has even developed along the years a social doctrine on such matters as family, respect for life, rights and duties of citizens, the social obligations of the rich, relations between employees and employers, and so on.

A religious believer who meets another believer is not expected to behave as if there were no differences between what their religions demand in human conduct. That would be unrealistic. It would also be a refusal to share and to give witness.

Some religions even have instructions on when and where their followers should pray, or fast, or give alms, or make pilgrimages. Some religions prescribe what dress their followers or their ministers should wear during or outside worship. A Muslim should not be considered odd for praying at one corner of the international airport if his religion so prescribes at that time. The same thing applies to fasting during the month so indicated.

Religious dress needs special mention because it does attract considerable attention. Where there is no violation of the just laws of a country, a believer should not imagine that interreligious courtesy forbids him or her to put on the ordinary dress normal to that religion. If other believers resent this, they are being unreasonable. I shall never forget when I visited a beautiful Buddhist monastery in a hilly forest in Taiwan. It was a hot day. I traveled the two-hour car drive in black clerical dress. When I reached the monastery I changed to a Catholic bishop's white cassock, pectoral cross, ring, and all. I spent about three happy hours with the Buddhist master and his disciples, monks, and nuns. At the moment of leaving to catch a train for my next stop, I changed back to my black clerical dress. The master and his monks and nuns did not hide their disappointment.

They asked me: "Where is that nice white garment of yours?" And sure enough when the master and two of the disciples visited me in Rome a year afterward, they unmistakably wore their yellow *kasaya*.

The point I want to make is that interreligious courtesy does not require of a Catholic priest or religious sister, a Muslim sheik, a Buddhist monk, a Shinto priest, or a Sikh to hide one's religious identity in the way one dresses. To dress in the way that is normal in one's religion is not regarded as a provocation. To try to hide one's identity in dress could cause suspicion.

Religious Identity in Celebrations

Every organized religion has some celebrations that are particular to it. These celebrations vary in their degree of importance and in the relative solemnity attached to them within that religion.

The Jews, for example, celebrate *Rosh Hashanah* (first of the year) and *Yom Kippur* (the Day of Atonement), which comes ten days after, as well as other feasts.

Catholics celebrate the Incarnation of the Son of God (the feast of Jesus' becoming man), Jesus' Nativity at Christmas, His suffering, death, resurrection, and ascension at Easter, the descent of the Holy Spirit on the early Church on Pentecost Day, the feast of the Most Blessed Trinity, the feast of the Body and Blood of Christ, the feasts of the Immaculate Conception and Assumption of the Blessed Virgin Mary, and the feast of All the

Saints. Catholics also celebrate jubilees connected with Christ.

The Muslims celebrate *Id al-Adha* or *Id al-Kabir* (feast of the Sacrifice of Abraham), *Id al-Fitr* or *Id al-Saghir* (feast of the Breaking of the Fast), and *Mawlid al-Nabi* (birthday of Muhammad).

The Hindus have *Diwali* (feast of lamps) and *Maha Shiva Ratri* (feast in God's honor).

The Theravada Buddhists celebrate *Vesakh* (in honor of Buddha's birth, enlightenment, and passing away) and the Mahayana Buddhists celebrate *Nirvana* Day (anniversary of Buddha's passing away).

The Shintoists and many of the Traditional Religionists celebrate a yearly feast in honor of their ancestors. One could go on naming feasts in other religions.

Interreligious dialogue does not ask a religious community to suppress its identity in its celebrations. It is not an offense to other religions to carry out a ritual that expresses the belief of one's religion. Indeed, a religion would endanger its permanence in its beliefs and practices, or at least weaken its coherence as a religious community, if it did not have occasional celebrations of the major pillars of belief that give meaning to it and hold it together.

The spirit of interreligious relations would suggest that some suitable form of invitation to other believers be considered at such celebrations. But no hard and fast rule should be entertained. There are religions that consider a celebration so particular to their "family" that the presence, let alone the active participation, of people who do not belong to that faith community cannot be considered. Every religion should strive to be true to itself.

I say all this because I have, for example, seen some Catholics who are so enthusiastic about interreligious relations that they get unnecessarily preoccupied with inviting other believers to the Eucharistic celebration, and someone has even asked if these cannot be invited to receive Holy Communion. Catholic doctrine and practice appreciate the advantage of inviting other believers to the Eucharistic celebration at occasions like marriages, funerals, anniversaries, local and national feasts, and whenever neighborly and friendly relations so advise. But the reception of Holy Communion is understood as a ritual act reserved exclusively to the Catholic community of faith, and even within it, only to members who fulfill certain conditions. It is the duty of Catholics who invite their friends of other religions to the Eucharistic celebration to explain this so that no offense may be taken where none is intended.

There is another way in which believers in one religion can show goodwill toward other believers who are celebrating a religious feast. They can send them a goodwill message. They can tell them to what extent the major belief or practice underlined in that celebration may be reflected in the other religion. The Pontifical Council for Interreligious Dialogue, for example, has since 1967 been sending a Message to the Muslims of the world during their month of fasting each year. This annual Message, now in its thirtieth edition, gathers a growing number of feedback messages and expressions of gratitude. From 1995 the Pontifical Council began to send a similar Message to Hindus during their celebration of *Diwali* and to Buddhists at the feast of *Vesakh*. Some Muslims send messages to Christians at Christmas and New Year's Day.

While every religious family has the right to retain its identity in its religious celebrations, it is also to be accepted that if one loves a person, one rejoices with that person when he or she celebrates a feast. The practical question is to agree on a mutually acceptable form that such a gesture should take.

Necessity of Religious Self-Image

The above considerations help to see how necessary it is for a dialogue partner to have a clear religious self-image. Unless one knows clearly who one is and what one stands for, then the meeting with others is neither advisable nor safe. A country chooses as ambassador one of its citizens who is a credit to the country. It does not send as envoy to another country a citizen who does not know the name of the country's president, who cannot distinguish the country's flag from a lineup of four flags, who has no courage to identify what country he or she came from, and who does not like the national dress where such exists. A dialogue person is in a sense an ambassador.

Let it be repeated that quiet presentation of one's religious identity is not a form of provocation. It is not aggression. It is not intolerance. It is not fanaticism. It is simply being who and what one is, and meeting others in all honesty, sincerity, truth, and courage. If the dialogue partner wants one to hide or lose one's religious identity card as a condition for dialogue, then such a demand is unreasonable. It will also be found in practice that believers who make such demands are generally not open to dialogue.

Religious believers therefore — Christians, Jews, Muslims, Hindus, Buddhists, Sikhs, Traditional Religionists, and others — should in all sincerity meet one another as they are, present themselves without any masks, and strive to understand and accept one another, enrich one another, and work together to build a better society.

cHAPTEr
5

Possibility of

Doctrinal Dialogue

A PERSON WHO HAS FOLLOWED THESE PAGES THUS FAR MAY NOW reply: I grant that each religion should retain its identity when it meets other religions. But I have my doubts on doctrinal dialogue that you earlier called *dialogue of discourse*. Is dialogue of theological exchange really possible? Is it not wiser to concentrate on other forms of dialogue?

May I attempt an answer as follows?

Can Provoke Heated Debates

Some believers are opposed to dialogue on items of belief because they consider that such will easily provoke heated debates. Each partner in the dialogue would like to defend his or her religious beliefs and prove that these are right. Some may even suggest the superiority of their beliefs over those of others and try to detect flaws or errors in these others. The expected reaction of the others need not be calm and sweet. The temperature of the debate is likely to rise. Agreement is not likely.

A bitter taste could be left over from such an exercise. And no clear advantage can be detected. Therefore it seems prudent to avoid doctrinal debates.

The answer is that this risk exists, but it can be avoided. To begin with, dialogue of theological exchange is not a debate on religious beliefs to see which side wins. It is mutual listening. A partner who sets out to prove the other side wrong and inferior does not have an acceptable dialogical attitude, but rather the mentality of a religious debater or controversialist. A dialogue partner who is authentic wants to listen and understand, and then to contribute in the hope that the other side will reciprocate and will also be willing to listen and understand. And it must be noted that to understand need not mean to accept or to agree!

Moreover, it is psychologically unwise for two groups of believers to begin their interreligious contacts with a discussion of doctrine. They should begin with dialogue of life and dialogue of social works. It is only when friendship and trust have grown up between them, and if they are theologically well prepared, that it would be advisable for them to take on doctrinal differences.

Beliefs Too Dear for Discussion

Some religious beliefs can touch rather sensitive chords in the piety of the religious family in question. A discussion on such dogmas with people who do not accept them can be upsetting. Unintended hurt can easily be made on very delicate areas of religious belief. The risk of such beliefs being buffeted or desecrated in debate is even more frightening.

Examples for Muslims are the sacred nature and the divine origin of the Qur'an and the respect due to the prophet Muhammad. For Catholics one can think of the dogmas of the Most Blessed Trinity, of the Incarnation, of the Holy Eucharist, and of the Blessed Virgin Mary as the Mother of God.

Any lack of respect in the discussion of such beliefs is likely to upset the religious sensitivities of those to whom these beliefs are so dear. Therefore some people think that such beliefs should not be exposed in the rough and open market of academic interreligious discussion, as if they were articles for free buying and selling.

This objection has to be taken rather seriously. One does not promote good relations with other believers by walking carelessly among the delicate wares of their most cherished religious beliefs. Respect and observance of a sense of the sacred are part of the mentality and behavior pattern of a true religious believer.

When one meets other believers, it is important to listen carefully to what they say and to take note of how they feel. It is equally necessary to strive to appreciate what elements in their religion are considered more central than others by them. An iconoclastic or don't-care attitude or a demythologizing approach is sure to alienate and repel, and even to spell the end of dialogue. It is also unwise to delve into beliefs in the other religion that one does not well understand. Listening, silence, quiet reflection, and respectful attention will go a long way toward providing a viable solution.

Take It or Leave It

There are some believers who adopt a much more peremptory attitude toward doctrinal dialogue. They are convinced that their particular religious belief comes from a revelation from God that is final and irreversible. They do not see any room for any discussion. Other believers, they hold, should either take it or leave it. The most that such people would concede in meeting other believers is an opportunity to expose these beliefs so that others might accept them.

The answer is equally peremptory. If indeed a person looks on an interreligious encounter as a platform to convince others to accept that person's beliefs, then that person is not really engaged in dialogue but in an effort to spread his or her religion. This effort, as we shall see in the next chapter, is legitimate in itself. But it is not the same as interreligious dialogue.

Besides, even if one is fully convinced that one's belief is the final revelation from on high, it still pays to inform other believers about it in a dialogical spirit, to listen to their own exposition of their beliefs on such issues, to see if either side could not dispel prejudices of one kind or another on the matter from the other side, and even to ask oneself to what extent one has been able to internalize one's belief and to articulate it to others. It is therefore not acceptable that dialogue of theological exchange is a matter of "take it or leave it."

Promoting Mutual Communication

Thus it follows that when believers who are culturally and theologically well prepared do listen to one another on matters of belief, many positive advantages can be realized. The first benefit is that prejudices begin to fall. Caricatures and generalizations start being reduced in number and size. Here are some examples. When Muslims hear a reasoned statement of the Christian belief in three Persons in one God, the mystery indeed remains, but it does not now sound as absurd as it was believed before. That God the Father begot God the Son, receives better hearing when it is explained that the concept "beget" is not being used univocally as in human generation, since God does not have a body, but that the fact that we can analogically talk of begetting or conceiving a thought should make us more respectful and silent in front of this mystery. The procession of the Holy Spirit from the Father and the Son demands even more reverent attention. But a happy conclusion is that after several friendly and theologically well-informed expositions, questions, and answers, Muslims begin to see that Christians do not believe in three Gods but in one. Such a conclusion is most important and useful in promoting good interreligious relations, especially as the learned people who can engage in such elevated exchanges are generally in leadership positions, particularly in the academic world. They can do much to plant and water the seed of dialogue among the growing population and among those who are going to be journalists, teachers, politicians, business people, and lawyers.

Let us consider another example. Followers of Traditional Religions have been variously given such derogatory names as pagans, witch doctors, fetishists, or idolaters. These epithets indicate either a misunderstanding or no understanding of these religions. The word animist persists even today in describing these believers. The tag probably arose from the early European travelers who thought that these believers hold that trees, rivers, hills, and even lightning have souls. And they are believed to worship these souls. A dialogue of theological exchange with Traditional Religionists, or with exponents who are exact and factual in stating their beliefs, would have made clear that these people believe in one God, in nonhuman spirits good and bad, and in the human spirits of their ancestors. They may hold that there are spirits of rivers and hills and spirits of fertility and good harvest. But that does not justify calling them animists.

Better-informed contact with these religions may also show that some of their priests also engage in fortune-telling and in medical care through the wise use of herbs. But such activities are clearly seen by the Traditional Religionists to be separate from religious affairs. Moreover, the practitioners of such arts are not always religious figures. There are full-time fortune-tellers and professional herbalists or doctors. It is therefore not correct to label Traditional Religionists witch doctors. Only careful and patient dialogue of theological exchange can expose such generalizations.

Other examples can be mentioned. One needs to hear a Hindu professor in order to take another look at the usual judgment that Hindus are polytheists or pantheists. When one hears an orthodox Buddhist explain that Buddha did not speak about God but concentrated on what the individual should do in front of suffering and the passing nature of the things of this world, then one begins to understand more and more the Buddhist way of looking at reality.

Every religion has along the corridors of history accumulated a patrimony of beliefs, concepts, images, and spiritual panoramas, together with their expressions and manifestations even at the popular level. The better-prepared people of each religion who can articulate these beliefs and separate the essential from the nonessential, or even the extravagant and unorthodox, have the duty to do so. If they can do this across the interreligious dialogue table, it is all to the good, because they will thus be promoting interreligious good relations that go beyond initial courtesy.

Examples of Doctrinal Dialogue

The reader may now welcome hearing about some examples of doctrinal dialogue that have actually taken place.

I have already mentioned the initiative of the Groupe de Recherches Islamo-Chrétien, which is a collaborative study by Muslims and Christians on matters of belief. The fact that this group has produced a joint book on the Bible and the Qur'an, another on faith and justice, and a third on religion and society, is proof that joint reflection is not impossible.

In 1985 the Pontifical Council for Interreligious Dialogue (then called Secretariat for Non-Christians) organized a colloquium on Holiness in Christianity and in Islam. Each major topic was presented by a Christian and then by a Muslim, from their respective religious viewpoints. A participant of the other religion gave a written reaction. Then there was general discussion.

In 1990 representatives of the World Islamic Call Society held a meeting with representatives of the Pontifical Council for Interreligious Dialogue and of the Congregation for the Evangelization of Peoples. The topic was Mission and Da'wah (the call to Islam). The discussions turned on the motivations for spreading one's faith, the methods regarded as unacceptable, and the obstacles encountered.

In various years between 1989 and 1996 the Pontifical Council for Interreligious Dialogue and the Royal

Academy for Islamic Civilization Research, Al Albait Foundation in Jordan, have jointly organized colloquia between Christian and Muslim experts on topics such as the Rights of the Child, Religious Education, Women in Society, Religion and Nationalism, and Religion and the Use of the Earth's Resources. Although the topics were mainly social, elements of belief did come in. Such platforms help to build bridges between believers.

In 1995 there was an international colloquium between Christians and Buddhists on such matters as ideas on Christ and on Buddha and on their attitude toward the things of this world. One of the proofs of the usefulness of such contacts is that a leading Buddhist nun from the Taiwanese monastery in which the colloquium was held has written to me on several occasions to express her satisfaction and also her desire that such meetings should continue. When one reflects on the wide difference between Christianity and Buddhism, it becomes more convincing to say that dialogue of theological exchange is not impossible. What has already happened and is happening is possible. Even more, it is helpful, if rightly carried out.

cHAPTeR
6

Dialogue and the Propagation of One's Own Religion

LET US NOW FACE A CRUCIAL QUESTION THAT WORRIES MANY PEOPLE with reference to interreligious dialogue.

Stating the Question

People ask whether the practice of interreligious dialogue can be reconciled with the right of every believer to propose his or her religion to others, with a view to their accepting it and embracing it. Do interreligious good manners not discourage the commitment to share one's religion with others? Is such hesitation not dangerous to a missionary commitment? Does such mentality not seem to be telling missionaries that what matters is to be friendly to other believers, and not to increase the number in one's own religious household?

Conversely, it is asked whether a zealous missionary who preaches in order to win converts can sincerely and honestly be engaging in interreligious dialogue at the same time. Could such a missionary not be regarded as being two-faced? If one is sincere in proclaiming one's faith to others, could that person not be regarded as having a hidden agenda if at the same time he or she wants to engage in dialogue?

In short, it is asked whether dialogue and propagation of one's religion can coexist, and if so, what relationship can be established between them.

The Right to Propagate One's Religion

Let us begin by declaring that no matter how fervently we may wish to promote interreligious good relations, we must acknowledge the right of every believer to propose his religion to others with the hope that they may welcome it, believe in it, and embrace it. A believer who has internalized his or her religion is expected to love it and to make it a way of life. The next thing that one would expect from such a person is that the person would want to share that religion, that faith, that way of life, with others. We should not be blamed if we suspect a believer who did not want to share his or her faith with others. We would then like to ask several questions. Is the person really convinced of it? Does the person consider that religion a good thing? If so, is that religion regarded as valid for all, or is it considered a family or hereditary patrimony?

I grant that all religions are not equally missionary. There are some that are so tied up with racial, ethnic, or national elements in their origin and history that their followers do not feel a great urge to spread them beyond their usual frontiers. However, there are also religions that regard their message as not only valid for all but also as meant for all humanity. And they regard their followers as having not only the right but also the duty to proclaim their religion worldwide. What we cannot deny to our fellow human being is the right to strive to share one's religion with people. There are, however, conditions that are acceptable, and others that are not.

Proselytism

Proselytism is generally taken to mean the effort to spread one's religion by methods that are regarded as unacceptable. Examples of such methods are taking advantage of the poor by giving them money or other gifts in exchange for conversion, and exerting political or social pressure on people to get them to embrace a particular religion in order to avoid harassment, or boycott, or even violence, or in order to gain promotion or business contracts. It is also proselytism to induce people to convert to a religion because of their ignorance or lack of economic development. Of course, deceit and physical pressure are ways of carrying out proselytism.

All such methods deserve condemnation. The human person has an innate God-given dignity that deserves respect. Religion should be proposed, not imposed. Religious affiliation or unity in belief arrived at as a result of pressure — be that pressure physical, psychological, political, economic, social, or otherwise —

is not worthy of the human person. It insults the person on whom it is exerted. It is ignoble of the one who applies such pressure. It does not do honor to God to whom all true religious acts are directed.

Religion should flow freely from the human heart as a free response of the human creature to God the Creator. Therefore the effort to share one's religion should respect the human dignity of the other person, the right of others to freedom in matters religious, and the individual responsibility that every human being should have toward God.

There is, however, a use of the word proselytism that is unacceptable. Some people use the word to refer to every effort to propose one's religion to others, even when the methods used are noble, honest, and respectful. It is wrong and confusing to use the term in this sense. It is like giving a dog a bad name in order to hang it. It is like wanting to deny and to condemn the right of a person to share one's religion. This fundamental human right should never be denied anyone. It is therefore wrong for the followers of a majority religion in a country to outlaw all other religions and regard all their initiatives to spread themselves as proselytism.

Dialogue Is Not the Same as Propagation of One's Religion

While we hold firm to the right of a believer to share his or her faith, provided that the means adopted are acceptable, we must at the same time add that this activity is not the same as interreligious dialogue. They have two different aims, or formal objects, or ends, or goals. Dialogue aims at meeting a believer of a different religious conviction in order to listen, to understand, to be enriched, and to cooperate for the good of society. Dialogue presupposes that each partner has a clear and peaceful religious identity.

Missionary effort to propose one's religion to other believers, or to nonbelievers, on the other hand, aims at the conversion of the other persons to one's religious conviction. It is marked by proclamation, teaching, catechesis, supply of information and books, invitation to celebrations of the religious community, introduction into its history and patrimony, together with information on the advantages of belonging to that religious community.

Both activities, proclamation and dialogue, are good and legitimate. But they are not the same. One is not a means to the other.

Conversion to Another Religion Is Not the Aim of Dialogue

It is important for all who engage in interreligious dialogue to accept that such dialogue does not aim at convincing the other person to embrace the religion of the dialogue partner.

If indeed conversion to the other religion were to

be the formal object, or aim, of dialogue, then we would be faced with two alternatives. Either such an aim would be declared or it would not. If the aim was so declared, then it would be the end of dialogue, because the other person would predictably walk away. And if the person did not then walk away but freely accepted to be instructed in the other religion, then we would now be dealing not with dialogue but with religious catechesis prior to reception into the other faith community.

If, on the other hand, conversion to the other religion was the aim of dialogue but was not declared to the interlocutor, then we have a case of religious smuggling. It would be a case of a believer trying to win a convert by dishonestly hiding his or her real intentions. This is one of the cases that should be labeled proselytism. It is unworthy both of the proponent and of the hoodwinked partner. Authentic dialogue, on the contrary, is marked by honesty, sincerity, nobility, and simplicity. Smuggling is disapproved both by customs officials and by true dialogue promoters.

Conversion to God Is Needed for Dialogue

There is, however, a sense in which we can rightly speak of conversion as a needed mental state and as a result of dialogue. It is in the sense of greater conversion to God. Every believer who meets other believers in interreligious contacts should strive to be more and more open to the action of God. God can speak to us through our encounter with other believers. Such can become occasions in which we are challenged to become more faithful to the deeper calls of our faith. Contact with the self-discipline of Theravada Buddhist monks, for example, can challenge a Catholic to fast more, to smoke less, to go more against the current of a consumer culture, and to consider taking the vow of celibacy in the religious life or in another form of the consecrated life.

After our initial conversion to God, every one of us can, and should, make progress in our lives of dedication to God. Interreligious contacts, while not being the chief means to promote this, can help in such continuing conversion.

A necessary requirement is that the dialogue participant should not close the heart to God's action but should on the contrary be open and willing to go where the divine light leads. Indeed, this is a necessary requirement for fruitful dialogue, if dialogue is not to be reduced to a dry college debate that just trains one in the art of making arguments. Willingness to follow the light will thus include readiness to admire all that is good, noble, true, or holy in the other religion, to rejoice about its existence, and to praise God for it.

Earlier I asserted the right of the human person to religious freedom, in the sense that no one, whether individual, government, or organization, should use force on a person in matters religious. Now I must add that everyone is bound before God sincerely to look for the truth in religious matters. And having found the truth, the person is bound before God to embrace it. Otherwise the person is running away from the truth, from the light. The person would then not be leaving the heart open for divine action and guidance. Continuing conversion to God is a requirement for every genuine believer, and therefore also for believers who engage in interreligious contacts.

Can such contacts sometimes become the occasion in which one is persuaded that God is calling the person to pass over to the other religion? We cannot exclude this *a priori*. We cannot make rules for God's action in us. If a believer came to such a conclusion, prayer, reflection, and asking wise and honest believers for counsel would be required.

If a Catholic were ever to find himself or herself in such an unlikely situation, a good theologian would remind the person of the teaching of the Church on salvation and belonging to the Church, especially as explained in *Lumen Gentium*, 14. The individual should be aware that conscience has to be guided by correct doctrine, and for a Catholic this is received through the teaching authority of the Church. But the principle remains valid that every individual will finally stand before God's judgment seat to answer for all life's choices. What must not be done is to use force to get a person to go against conscience, because that would be to deprive that person of the exercise of the fundamental human right to freedom of religion.

From this reflection, it follows that it is not right to punish a person with social excommunication, deprivation of rights as a citizen, or even threats of physical violence or death, just because the person, following conscience, decides to pass over to another religion. Societies or religions that apply such measures, even in the world of today, need far-seeing leaders and reformers who will help them to appreciate that this is not the proper way to treat human persons. There should be no compulsion in matters of conscience. In matters religious, every individual should be allowed to exercise responsibility toward God the Creator and Judge, with full openness to the divine action, and with personal responsibility for the consequences of failing to say yes to God's light and guidance.

Relationship Between Proclamation and Dialogue

The reader by now must have drawn the conclusion that if interreligious dialogue is not opposed to the effort to spread one's religion, and yet is not identified with it, then there must be some relationships between the two activities. Indeed there are.

If I want to preach my faith to others with the hope that they may eventually accept it and embrace it, then it is better for me and for those people that I should know their religious background and culture as well as possible. As those people do not come from a religious and cultural void, the better I understand their background, the greater hope can be nourished that I shall be able, in my case, to present to them a Christianity that will take root on local soil, and a Christianity that will show appreciation for all the elements that are good, true, noble, or holy from their religious and cultural heritage. This touches the whole issue of inculturation about which the Catholic Church, for example, is so engaged today. The Gospel should become incarnate among peoples and cultures and not look like a foreigner with passport and visa for limited stay.

Interreligious dialogue helps very much to promote such inculturation because it promotes mutual knowledge between the religions of the dialogue partners. And since religion and culture have close ties, the interaction between dialogue and proclamation is considerable. If, therefore, a missionary wants to bring another religion to the Thai, the missionary should know Buddhism and Thai culture. If you want to evangelize the Ashanti people of Ghana, you should know African Traditional Religion and Ashanti culture. If you want to bring the Gospel to the Indonesians, you had better know Islam and Indonesian culture. This can be applied to other religions and peoples.

Another reason why a missionary should be an expert in interreligious dialogue is that proclamation should be dialogical, not monological. The person who receives the preaching of a new religion is not passive. The person is expected to listen, to reflect, to react, and to ask questions. Even when the person decides to embrace the new faith, many processes will still have to go on by way of making the new faith personally received and authentically lived. The entire religious and cultural past of the receiver of the new faith comes into play. Respect for the person who receives the new faith argues in favor of collaboration between dialogue and proclamation.

Interreligious dialogue, on the other hand, is promoted, not hindered, when there is free proclamation. If everyone had the same religion, there would be neither need nor room for interreligious dialogue. Freedom to practice one's religion and freedom to preach it should lead a person to accept the fact of religious plurality and therefore to be in favor of dialogue. While no one should promote a multiplication of religions as if a supermarket of religions were the ideal place for dialogue, it is quite another matter whether force should be used to compel a person to embrace one religion rather than another. It has been argued above that this would be totally wrong and unacceptable. Given, therefore, the freedom to share one's religion, dialogue is helped, not impeded, by the missionary effort of other believers.

Another consideration that shows the interaction between proclamation and dialogue is the need to respect the truth, and eventually to respect God, the fountain of all truth. In the various religions, people are seeking answers to the fundamental questions that concern human existence: the origin of man, the essence of happiness, the reason for moral evil or sin, the explanation for suffering, what happens to man after death, and especially about the Being that explains all other beings as their Creator. Some valid answers that the human mind, not without divine help, has found to these tormenting questions have been handed down in some form by the major world religions. It is part of our respect for God and for truth that wherever we find elements of these valid answers, we acknowledge them and give thanks to God for them. Sincere interreligious dialogue does this. Humble proclamation of one's religion acknowledges this. The two activities are tributes to God, the origin of every truth who never contradicts Himself.

Reciprocity

It was argued above that the human person has the right to freedom of religion. This includes the liberty to practice one's religion and also to share it with others. This right applies both to individuals and to groups or to religious communities. Since it is a right that is inherent in human nature, as coming from God, it follows the same human being everywhere. It is therefore valid in every country, culture, or region.

Some examples may serve to illustrate the point. Italy has been traditionally Catholic. So have Ireland and Spain. But Jews, Muslims, Hindus, and Buddhists are not forbidden to live in these countries, to practice their religion there, and even to propose it to citizens of those countries, as long as they adopt acceptable methods. This is the principle of religious freedom as a fundamental human right.

By the same token, such a right should be applicable to Catholics, and indeed to other Christians and other believers, in countries where Islam, Hinduism, Buddhism, or some other religion is that of the majority. This is what reciprocity is all about.

It is regrettable that even at this end of the second millennium, there are still some religions and countries that do not welcome this principle. They would like to exploit the freedom of religion that exists in other countries in order to spread their religion. But in some countries in which their religion is that of the majority, they will not allow other religions to grow, or they curtail their activities within very narrow limits. The world is waiting for great men and women to influence these situations in favor of freedom of religion and reciprocity in relationships.

cHAPTEr
7

Theological Reasons for the Engagement of the Catholic Church in Interreligious Dialogue

MANY OF THE READERS OF THIS BOOK MAY BE CATHOLICS OR OTHER Christians. Others may be Jews, Hindus, Buddhists, Muslims, Sikhs, Traditional Religionists, or followers of other religions. All may want to know why the Catholic Church in particular is engaged in interreligious dialogue. May I state in my own words the theological reasons as I see them?

Same God the Creator of All

The same God created all men and women. There is only one God. He is the Maker of heaven and earth. The human being is His masterpiece among all the visible creatures in the world.

There is not a separate God for the Christians and another God for the Muslims or the Buddhists. It is the same God who created every human being.

Moreover, this God is a provident God. He has provided people with water and light, air and heat, rivers and oceans, valleys and mountains, trees and herbs, crops and cereals, birds and animals. It is the Creator who made the seasons and who sees that rain keeps the earth verdant.

This provident God knows each human being by name. No man or woman is just a number before Him. Each is an individual person for whom He has a plan with all its details.

My faith also teaches me that God loves men and women. It was out of His loving magnanimity that He freely created each of us. He wants each of us to enter into a relationship of love with Him. He is our Father and we are His children. When therefore we call one another brothers and sisters, we are not engaging in metaphorical language. We are not indulging in a baseless ideological expression. We are stating a reality. And all this applies to every human being, even before one considers to what religion he or she belongs or does not belong.

Human Nature the Same in All

The unity of human nature was considered in an earlier chapter as one of the reasons in favor of interreligious dialogue by all believers. Now it needs to be examined more closely as a theological reason impelling the Catholic Church to engage in this exercise.

The provident and loving God has given the same

human nature to every man and woman. All human beings have a certain basic equality and dignity as persons, irrespective of their cultural, educational, or religious background.

Each human being feels the need to grow, to know, to love, and to be loved. Every man or woman is created a social being with a tendency toward association with others. Indeed, every human being needs other human beings in order to develop, to grow, and to reach the height of his or her potential.

The human soul is gifted by God with a thirst for the truth and a seeking for happiness. Both thirsts can in the final analysis be satisfied by God alone. The human soul, in short, is searching for God, and the human heart will never find rest until its rests in God. This is an indication of the Christian belief that all men are called to a common final destiny: the fullness of life in God, initially in this world by grace, and permanently in the next in the beatific and eternal vision of God as He is in heaven.

Religion is a desire of the human heart. There may be, and have been, mistakes in man's religious search. But the quest of how best to relate to the Creator is not only correct. It is also innate and unquenchable in man, as atheistic totalitarian systems have realized after doing much damage to man for decades.

People also appreciate association with others in the expression of their religious belief and worship and in the living of their lives according to their religion. It is very much in the nature of man to have organized religion, and not just individual religious beliefs and practices.

These facts about God the Creator and about the nature of man, which apply to everyone irrespective of religious affiliation, are already a firm foundation for the Catholic Church's engagement in interreligious relations. But there are yet deeper theological reasons that are a result of express revelation from God, and not just a matter of natural theology that can be arrived at by pure reason. Here are some of them.

Jesus Christ the Savior of All

My faith tells me that when the first man and woman, Adam and Eve, offended God, He did not abandon humanity in its fallen state. God promised a savior. For centuries, through the prophets, He taught man to hope for salvation.

In the fullness of time, the Eternal Father sent his only Son as the Savior of all humanity. God thus decided to come into human history to save man. Jesus Christ, the Son of God, took on human nature in the womb of the Virgin Mary by the power of the Holy Spirit, and was born in Bethlehem. After about thirty years of private life in Nazareth, He gathered disciples, inaugurated the Kingdom of God with His preaching and miracles, and finally freely suffered, died on the Cross, and rose again on the third day as He had earlier promised.

By His Incarnation (that is, His becoming man), Jesus Christ was somehow uniting Himself with every human being. Aware that He came to save all, He was taking on Himself the punishment due for the sins of every man and woman. He was making it possible for every man and woman to be associated with Him in His mystery of suffering, death, and resurrection so that everyone would profit from the redemption that He won for all. Just as in Adam all men and women became members of a fallen race, so in Christ, by a type of mystical and spiritual solidarity, all men and women are to find life, to become reconciled with God, and to have the possibility to become members of the new family of God.

My faith tells me that Jesus Christ died on the Cross not just for Christians but for every single human being, "to gather together the scattered children of God" (Jn 11:52). His love went out to all humanity. He spread His arms on the Cross as a symbol of His all-embracing love.

Many believers have in practice not heard of Christ. But through a sincere practice of what is good in their religion, and by following the dictates of their conscience, they can be concretely responding to God's offer of salvation in Jesus Christ, even while they do not know or accept Him as their Savior. To enter the Church expressly, however, would give them a more abundant share in the means to salvation.

Here is where the Church comes in.

Christ Sent the Church for All

When Jesus Christ was on earth, He gathered twelve Apostles, seventy-two disciples, and a wider circle of followers who were often with Him. They were the nucleus of the Church that He instituted and sent on a universal mission. He said to the Apostles: "As my Father sent me, I also send you" (Jn 20:21).

Christ sent His Church to bring His Good News of salvation to every man and woman until the end of the world. The Church was not to reject any of them. For those who accept the Message, believe in Christ, receive Baptism, and enter the Church, Christ promises faith, hope, and charity, regenerated life that He won for all by His passion and death, the richness of the sacramental life in the Church, and the help of the Christian community so that they can be good citizens of both the earthly city and of the heavenly city. To those who do not accept faith in Christ and Baptism into the Church, the Church that Christ founded is nevertheless to offer the message of justice, reconciliation, unity, and love, as well as her readiness for mutual understanding, collaboration, and solidarity, to make this world a happier place in which to live. And this will come nearer to possibility, the more people live according to God's will.

Christ sent His Church to be a sign and instrument that promotes union with God and unity between peoples. The Church has primarily a religious and spiritual mission, not one of a political or economic nature. The Church has the assignment to remind people of that transcendent Being who is God, Creator, Providence, and Father of all. The Church is to help people raise their eyes and hearts to God, strive to know more about Him and His will for human beings, and make an effort to respond to His love and live according to His will.

Toward human beings, the Church has the assignment of promoting mutual knowledge and acceptance in the midst of differences; readiness to discuss, to reconcile, and to forgive rather than to resort to violence; willingness to work together to face many problems and challenges that they could not solve single-handedly; and finally openness to love one another as Christ has loved us and shown it by freely laying down His life for us all. The Church believes that the more men and women know about Christ, the more they will know about themselves and their high calling, and the better they will be able to function as a family of peoples. This is not an empty dream. This can, and should, become a reality.

The Catholic Church also sees it as her duty to promote the authenticity of the various peoples on earth, together with their cultures, and to favor a healthy unity in diversity, as the various peoples praise

God with what they are and have. Therefore even when people of differing cultures embrace the Christian faith and receive Baptism, the Church wants them to bring along with them the positive elements of their cultures and religious backgrounds. They will thus be able to pray, sing, and worship in one community of faith and love, while not denying their native authenticity as various peoples.

Anyone who reflects on the implications of the above can see that these reasons give the Church no option but to seek to meet every human being, and therefore also to be involved in interreligious relations. But there are also positive reasons arising out of actual contacts across religious frontiers.

What the Church Learns Through Dialogue

Through contact with other believers, the Church also learns much. Christians learn what great gifts — for example, of wisdom, holiness of life, love of others, self-gift to others, and asceticism — God has given to some people who are outside the visible boundaries of the Church. Deeply religious books, centuries of monastic life marked by celibacy, poverty, and quest for transcendence, elements of grace and truth, and excellent progress in human virtues are all among what interreligious contacts have actually allowed the Church to discover among some other believers. Of course, I am not suggesting that most of the other believers have reached these heights. But what cannot be denied, by anyone who has had enough contact with them, is that some of them *de facto* do attain such a stature.

And wherever there is authentic prayer or love of others, we should believe that God is somehow at work there. It is not necessary for us to understand how God can give His gifts and His grace. The Spirit blows where He wills.

I shall never forget when I met a Muslim holy man who lived on his own outside Faisalabad in Pakistan in 1988, or when I met a Tendai Buddhist abbot in Kyoto in 1987 and 1992. They spoke words of wisdom. They dressed simply. They lived frugally. They radiated love of others. The Muslim showed great attention to God. The Buddhist manifested admiration for the Pope and the Catholic Church and a desire to work with Catholics to make this world a better place for all. I praised God for the workings of His grace.

Contact with other believers can encourage ecumenism among Christians. It helps Christians to realize better that their divisions are an obstacle to inter-religious relations because the other believers see that Christians do not speak with one voice. If all Christians were united in one fold and under one shepherd, if they all made a united approach to the followers of other religions, their joint witness to Christ would gain in credibility, their cooperation with other believers in joint projects would be stronger, and the solution to many social and cultural challenges and problems would be more permanent.

In interreligious dialogue, the Church learns how Christians can cooperate with other believers in order to seek to eliminate discrimination against people because of their color, language, sex, or religion. Moreover, tension in society and between nations, terrorism, violence and war, the painful phenomenon of refugees and displaced persons, the many problems facing the family, harmony among people, and, in general, development, justice, and peace demand the joint attention of all believers.

As if to underline the necessary contribution that religion can make toward solving these problems, Pope John Paul II, during the International Year for Peace in 1986, invited representatives of most of the religions of the world to come to Assisi to fast and pray for peace. And the response was very enthusiastic. Catholics, as I have already remarked, take part in the World Conference on Religion and Peace. In this multireligious organization they are able to work with believers from across a wide range of religions to tackle some of the tasks named above.

No matter the many serious differences between Christianity and Islam, it has been possible for followers of both religions to work together to defend family values on specific points during the 1994 United Nations Cairo Conference, as was already noted above.

When, therefore, I said in earlier pages that believers can cooperate to promote human culture, justice, development, love, and peace, I was not just enunciating a theory. I was saying what has also been happening.

In meeting peoples of other religions and cultures, the Church can be challenged in a positive way regarding the manner of expressing her faith and carrying out her worship. It is true that the contents of the faith do not change. But it is also true that the meeting of the philosophical systems that underlie the other religions has been enriching for the Church. This, of course, implies long and patient study and loving but careful sifting. It is necessary to avoid facile solutions and hurried adaptations that may later be found unsuitable, or even harmful. But there is no doubt that Christianity, which for centuries has articulated her belief in a Greco-Roman cultural environment, has gained by contact with religions and philosophies from Asia and Africa.

Similar remarks can be made about cultural elements from the various continents. Contact with them compels the heralds of the Good News of Jesus Christ to study how the Gospel can be given a local expression while remaining unchanged. The flexibility and variety in liturgical celebration that have been tested and approved in parts of Africa and Asia are witnesses to this positive impact. Those who have witnessed the Mass of the Roman Rite as approved for Zaire cannot fail to see in it the African contribution of color, joy at celebration, congregational participation, and reasonable body movement. Similar elements were visible in St. Peter's Basilica at the opening and closing Masses of the African Synod in 1994. When I took part in Masses celebrated in India, I was struck by the simplicity of the setting, the gentle but deep significance of the gestures, and the high visibility given to flowers and incense.

These are but a few examples of what I mean when I say that the Church can learn through contact with other religions and cultures. And she can be enriched in her efforts at inculturation of the Gospel message.

Catholic Church Committed to Interreligious Dialogue

For all the above-stated theological reasons, the Catholic Church is deeply committed to interreligious dialogue. Of course, the Church preaches Christ and regards it as the apex of her mission to proclaim that in Jesus Christ, the one mediator between God and man (cf. 1 Tim 2:4-6), the fullness of religious truth and salvation is offered to every man and woman, and that there is no salvation in any other name. At the same time, the Church is convinced that interreligious relations are part and parcel of what she is sent for.

It is remarkable that the Second Vatican Council (1962-1965), the largest gathering of Catholic bishops at any time in history, with a very clear image of what the Church is and what her mission is, emphasized the necessity to proclaim the Good News of Christ in its missionary decree *Ad Gentes*, but at the same time issued *Nostra Aetate*, its declaration on interreligious dialogue. Moreover, the Council continued to inculcate the necessity of Christians working with other believers, and indeed with all people of good will, in its pastoral constitution, *Gaudium et Spes*. The message is highly coherent, convincing, and workable, as the last thirty years have shown.

The Pontifical Council for Interreligious Dialogue, the dicasterial organ set up in 1964 to promote this vision, has articulated many of these convictions in two policy statements: *The Attitude of the Church towards the Followers of other Religions: Reflections and Orientations on Dialogue and Mission,* issued in 1984, and *Dialogue and Proclamation: Reflections and Orientations on Interreligious Dialogue and the Proclamation of the Gospel of Jesus Christ,* in 1991. The latter document was significantly published conjointly with the Congregation for the Evangelization of Peoples, the dicasterial organ for the spread of the Faith.

Practical proof of the commitment of the Catholic Church to interreligious relations can be seen also from the activities during these thirty years of the Popes, of the Pontifical Council for Interreligious Dialogue, of the Church at diocesan and national and even continental levels, of religious orders and congregations, and of Catholic universities, movements, and associations, as well as individuals. An unbiased observer will be convinced that this commitment of the Church to dialogue is neither marginal nor peripheral. It is seen more and more as part of the universal mission of the Church.

CHAPTER 8

Requirements for
Fruitful Dialogue

FROM THE ABOVE CONSIDERATIONS, IT IS CLEAR THAT INTERRELI-gious dialogue does not possess any magic power to produce the desired effects. If it is to produce good fruit, some requirements will have to be there. They are already implied in the above pages. But it will do no harm to list some of them here expressly.

Freedom in Society, Especially Religious Freedom

The climate in which interreligious dialogue grows and bears fruit is that of freedom. A society in which people cannot associate freely, nor meet when they wish, nor express their convictions and share their thoughts, is not conducive to interreligious relations.

Freedom of religion needs special mention. The individual should be free from compulsion in matters of conscience and religion, both in their practice and in sharing them with others. And every society, country, and region without exception should be willing to reciprocate and not to ask for freedom of religion for their coreligionists in one country, while denying the same right to other religious minorities in their own country.

Religious intolerance and extremism obviously make interreligious contacts difficult. The situation is made worse when political, racial, ethnic, and economic calculations come into the picture.

Clear Religious Identity

A partner in interreligious relations should have a clear religious identity. Such a person should be in good standing in his or her religious community, and not be a problem child. It is important that a prospective dialogue partner be firmly grounded in the traditions, beliefs, and practices of his or her faith community so that the person can, without danger to personal faith, meet other believers.

Conviction on Value of Dialogue

It sounds almost superfluous to say that if dialogue is to be fruitful, then the participants should first be convinced of its value. And yet there are people who still consider dialogue as reserved to specialists. There are others who suspect that it is a sign of some doubt about one's religion, or a symptom of weakness or lack of success in winning converts. A believer in another religion once said to me: "When you Catholics are no longer able to convert us, you now propose dialogue!" As long as people entertain such ideas, so long do they render themselves incapable of promoting meaningful interreligious relations.

Openness

The ideal dialogue partner needs to be open in many directions.

Toward God, a dialogue person should be open to the action of God's grace in him or her through the dialogue. This includes willingness to recognize and rejoice at the workings of God in people of other religions, and receptive minds regarding constructive values seen among other believers.

Toward other believers, openness includes readiness to revise preconceived ideas about them, ingrained prejudices, long-standing generalizations, and summary judgments. The open-dialogue partner is willing to be enriched by encounters with others and to admit possible mistakes or shortcomings by his or her coreligionists now, or in the past, without exaggerated self-defense or that attitude shown in the expression "My religious family is never wrong."

Love and Respect

It is not pious preaching to say that dialogue requires love of the dialogue partners and respect for them. If one does not really love, esteem, and respect a group, such an attitude will unfailingly transpire through the contacts, even when polite words are traded around. One who closes the heart against others also closes the door against fruitful exchange.

The one who loves is better able to understand, to be friendly, and to absorb the shock of a cold reception or a refusal to reciprocate. The friendly person knows how to wait in patience until the partner is ready to communicate. Temptations to become polemical or to pay the other person back in the same coin can then be resisted.

This attitude of love and respect includes the required adaptation to cultural differences and to the consequences of different levels of school education, as well as flexibility toward differing attitudes to punctuality, the answering of letters, and the keeping of promises. These are seemingly small matters; but I have seen non-attention to them ruining what could have been fruitful interreligious contacts.

Knowledge of the Other Religion

There comes a time in interreligious contacts when courtesy and a general knowledge of the other religion are no longer enough, and it now becomes necessary to know the religion of the dialogue partner at greater depth. This is particularly important for those who are in a leadership position. If one really wants to appreciate objectively the religion of the other, and not run the risk of misrepresenting it, then it will become necessary to give much more time to its study. I have seen believers rather hurt because dialogue partners with whom they had associated for a long time were still stating their belief in a way they found unacceptable.

The task is not always easy. Not all religious families are like the Catholic Church, which has a Congregation for the Doctrine of the Faith and a Magisterium (that is, teaching authority), vested in the Pope and in the bishops in communion with him. There are some religions where there are so many schools of thought and currents that it is hard to say exactly what that religion holds on a particular point.

To know what other religions hold and teach, it is advisable to read approved authors of that religion or to speak with them. However, at least for a Christian, it is also important to read a Christian author who is well versed in that religion but who can at the same time offer an acceptable Christian theological assessment of that religion from the standpoint of the Christian faith. This type of synthesis helps the nonexpert to know how best to dialogue with the believers in that other religion.

Formation of Leaders

In addition to deeper knowledge about other religions, it is also helpful, indeed practically necessary, that the major religions, that is, those that have many followers, should have a program of formation for leaders who will spearhead their dialogue initiatives. Such leaders cannot be improvised overnight. They are best chosen from among those who are interested in dialogue and who have shown reasonable competence.

The formation of such leaders should include academic training and practical exercise in the virtues most needed by dialogue people, especially listening, welcoming, being open, working with others, and being able to empathize, to love, and to wait. Initial minor assignments will help to prove the worth and ability of the trainees.

The major religions should not leave the direction of their dialogue efforts to private individuals or to self-appointed enthusiasts. Some way should be found to invest the official leaders of dialogue with this assignment and to let the religious community know about it. A time to monitor their performance should also be contemplated. All this leaves intact the possibility of initiatives springing from the imagination and gifts of individuals.

Healing Historical Memories

Some of the older religions have burdens of the past, which their followers today inherit from history and for which the present followers are not responsible. Some of these historical memories are loaded with misunderstandings, exaggerations, unclarified historical details, unhealed anger handed on from generation to generation, unjustified generalizations, and a forcing of the mentality of our times to ages gone by, when situations, sensitivities, and perceptions were rather different.

Famous among generally unhealed historical memories between Muslims and Christians are the crusades and the "holy wars," or *jihads*. Some Muslims would add colonization that was done in largely Muslim areas by countries of Western Europe, which some Muslims wrongly identify with Christianity. In some countries in Asia, memories of colonization and the promotion of Western-style Christianity can impede dialogue with some European Christians. To some extent, this may apply to parts of Africa. Historical memories between Hindus and Sikhs or between Muslims and Baha'is have not always been happy.

In all such cases, it is helpful for well-prepared representatives of the religions in question to meet, to seek patient historical unraveling of the facts as far as possible, and then to find their way to repentance, mutual asking for pardon, reconciliation, love, and unity. The solution cannot be to sweep the unhealed memories under the carpet. They will not disappear in that way. They will return repeatedly and haunt interreligious relations. The adequate response is to face them honestly, directly, and with hearts ready for truth and reconciliation.

Religious Apathy

Where there is no serious engagement in religion itself, no enthusiasm is to be expected in interreligious dialogue. People distracted by materialistic pursuits and weighed down by religious indifferentism cannot be expected to become convinced dialogue partners.

Our age is also marked by a multiplicity of sects and esoteric, pseudo-religious movements of many kinds. Some of them banalize and commercialize religion. A few of them present themselves as post-religious or supra-religious. A handful even want to be accepted as sent to unite all religions! Some of them directly attack one or other of the established religions. All of them create considerable confusion for people and thus make interreligious dialogue more difficult.

Of course, it would be unrealistic to want to see all the ideal requirements for dialogue concentrated in one place, person, or group of believers. Nevertheless, every believer can take a step toward rendering the climate a little less inhospitable.

cHAPTeR
9

Spirituality in Dialogue

DIALOGUE OF RELIGIOUS EXPERIENCE WAS MENTIONED IN AN EAR-
lier chapter as the fourth form of interreligious relations. As a type of spiritual energizing of all the other
chapters, it seems now useful to focus on spirituality in
dialogue, especially with reference to how the exercise
of dialogue should become a spiritual uplift for the person who engages in it.

Spirituality and Religion

Spirituality is related to religion. But they are not
the same thing. When we say spirituality, we generally
think of that dimension of the human being that gives
meaning and a sense of direction to human life. Spirituality calls on a person to go to the higher self and indeed
to go beyond self and aspire to some form of relationship with a Divine Being, or God.

Religion, on the other hand, conveys the idea of a
particular framework endowed with a belief system, a
moral code, a form of worship, and an authority struc-
ture to keep it together. Within a definite religion, people
find nourishment for the spiritual dimension of their

lives and carry on their spiritual pilgrimage in the company of others who hold the same faith.

There are close links between religion and spirituality, as can be seen from these tentative descriptions. Religion provides the wherewithal to live a spirituality, the vehicle for a spiritual journey. On the other hand, without the refined fuel that is spirituality, the vehicle that is religion would become a jumble of dry bones, well-arranged spiritual ironworks, or expertly put-together canonical laws that would nevertheless not be able to get going or keep going. Without the deep roots that spirituality supplies, religion would not be able to produce beautiful leaves and fruit.

Spirituality would normally exist in a religion. Within one religion, there can be several spiritualities. We think, for example, of the Franciscan spirituality, the Jesuit spirituality, the Benedictine spirituality, and the Dominican spirituality, all within the Catholic Church. These spiritualities are different ways or styles of living the same faith.

Some people may want to claim a spirituality for themselves, while they refuse to declare themselves members of any organized religion. I do not want to deprive them of this title, if what they mean is an effort of their soul to look for the transcendent, even when they say that they suspect all religions, or even that they know nothing of a transcendent Being, or when they go further and deny His existence. A possible interpretation of such "humanist spiritualities" is that they are really instances of the human soul looking for God without exactly knowing it.

Religion is the normal habitat of spirituality. And since this book is about dialogue between believers, we shall now move on, with an understanding of spirituality in the context of religion.

Necessity of Spirituality

As believers increase efforts and initiatives to meet one another, it is being more and more recognized that the contribution that spirituality can make is very important for interreligious dialogue. Knowledge of other religions, common projects, meetings, and techniques are good, but they are not enough.

The human soul is irrepressibly and incurably looking for the transcendent. While material things can bring a certain measure of satisfaction, they are soon recognized as insufficient. The human being is looking for contact with the Supreme Being, the Supreme Spirit, the Transcendent, the Absolute, the One who is Truth — in short, God.

There are riddles concerning human existence and the universe that cannot find an adequate answer in material terms: life, death, suffering, sin, earthquakes. There are desires of the human heart that cannot find final fulfillment in any creature: truth, love, peace, happiness.

The human being, when not weighed down, or crippled or blinded by earthly realities, wants to open out to transcendence, to another life after death, to immortality, to eternity, to the Infinite.

Most religions have throughout history developed ways of doing this. These various spiritualities are sometimes identified with some particular believers, or founders of religious movements, who have shown themselves gifted with special visions and missions on how to live their faith. And the fascination of their spiritualities has attracted disciples who cluster around their spiritual master to absorb and live that way of life.

It is most helpful to interreligious dialogue that those engaged in it be gifted with viable and, if possible, powerful spiritualities. They need not all be spiritual pillars and founders of religious congregations, institutes, movements, or associations. But they should be people who have sufficiently internalized their practice of this religion to such an extent that they live a marked spirituality. This is another way of saying that they should be deeply committed people in matters religious.

Quest for Holiness

God is totally other. He is apart from any creature. He dwells in light inaccessible. He is all truth, goodness, beauty, splendor, and love.

Fully aware that God is beyond us and above us, and that there is no other like Him, the human soul nevertheless aspires to have some contact with God. The desire to approach the Divinity is unquenchable in the human heart.

Various religions have expressed this quest in their own ways. Christians have their saints and mystics. Jews have their men of God and prophets. Muslims have their *sufi awliyá*. Hindus have their *rishis* and *sadhus*. Buddhists have their *arahant* (or *aarhat*). Followers of Traditional Religions have their spiritual guides and intermediaries with the Divine and the spirits.

For Christians, for example, holiness is the perfection of charity, which is the love of God that includes love of neighbor. Christians seek union with God through Jesus Christ, the Son of God-made-man. Jesus Christ is the key, the center, and the exemplar of the Christian quest for holiness. A Christian who wants to become holy strives to model life on Christ, to absorb His teachings, to live as He did and taught. In practice, the Christian meets Christ in and through the Church, by living a deeply committed life in the Church. Such a life will normally flower in the married state, or in the sacred priesthood, or in a form of consecrated life with vows, or as a single person. Most Christians are called to live their lives according to Christ in full involvement with secular affairs. Generally, it will be the case that one form of Christian spirituality will show itself in that person's life. For Christians, a holy person can be a mystic living as a hermit in the desert, or a monk or nun practicing contemplation in a monastery away from the public eye, or a busy bishop or priest. More often the holy person should be the diligent wife and mother, the dedicated hospital nurse or airline hostess, or the sought-after lawyer or eloquent politician. In the Christian concept, everyone, without exception, is called to holiness of life.

It will be interesting to hear our Jewish, Hindu, Buddhist, Muslim, Sikh, Zoroastrian, or Traditional Religionist friends tell us how holiness is understood and lived in their various religions. One thing is clear: The holier a person is, the more that person qualifies to engage in interreligious dialogue. Human beings will sooner meet one another if they first vertically seek union with God, with the Infinite, with the Transcendent, before they horizontally move to encounter one another. In God, who is truth and love, they are more likely to open up to one another, to understand one another, to love one another, and to study what they can do together, than if they ignored reference to God. This may explain why people who make a more-than-ordinary effort at holiness of life soon become friends even when they come from differing religions, languages, and cultures. Holiness of life is highly beneficial for the promotion of interreligious relations.

Sharing Spirituality in Dialogue

It was already argued above that in interreligious contacts the partners should retain their particular religious identities. After making due allowance for all the differences that exist between religions, one can say that experience has shown that it is profitable for dialogue partners to share their differing spiritualities.

To share in this case does not mean to embrace the other religion. But it must at least mean to listen, to try to understand, to ask questions, to admire what deserves admiration, and to allow oneself to be enriched by really good ideals, proved values, and precious patrimonies of humanity. With the necessary care, distinctions, and precaution, a sharing in philosophies and techniques can also be useful. But all this presumes that the participants are particularly well prepared, and are able to discern what could enrich them in their religion, and also the elements that would be altogether irreconcilable with their religions and spiritualities.

Christians, for example, may be surprised to find that some of their dialogue partners want to know more about Jesus Christ and about the Sermon on the Mount, which is like the manifesto of the Kingdom that Christ was inaugurating. Other believers want to know what makes the Catholic monastic orders tick, what explains the devotion of thousands of consecrated sisters to the service of the poor, why Catholic priests and religious embrace lives of consecrated celibacy, or even why Christ instructs Christians to turn the other cheek when a person strikes them on one cheek.

Just as the Christians share their spiritualities with

other believers, so will these be expected to share theirs with Christians. This is indeed dialogue at a deeper level than most people are accustomed to.

Advantages of Spirituality in Dialogue

Dialogue of spirituality will help all participants to have a rich spiritual nourishment for the other three forms of dialogue, namely, dialogue of life, dialogue of social action, and dialogue of theological exchange. Attention to the spiritual dimension will help to prevent these three types of dialogue from degenerating into external actions without much spiritual depth. A developed spirituality will spread its good effects over all the other initiatives of a dialogue partner, help them engage the whole person, and make them expressions and manifestations of a deeper life.

A Christian who engages in dialogue of spirituality with equally committed people of other religions is in a good position to admire the working of the Holy Spirit in them and to collaborate with such graces.

Exchange and sharing at this deep level — that of the spirit, combined with mutual witness to one's beliefs, religious convictions, rituals, and ascetical and meditational (or contemplative) practices — will go a long way to promote harmony, understanding, respect, and even love across religious frontiers.

I can cite as an example that the spiritual exchanges between Miss Chiara Lubich, founder of the Catholic

Focolare Movement, and Rev. Nikkyo Niwano, founder of the Buddhist Rissho Koseikai, have made possible and richer the friendship and communication between their two dynamic movements. Spiritual leaders of high stature can help unleash strong spiritual energy. Such interreligious communication and collaboration can help each participant to be more open to God's action for a continuing and greater conversion to God. Who does not see that for those who are able to arrive at such heights, all this is most helpful to spiritual progress? And for a religiously pluralistic society, this is good news indeed.

Spiritual Growth Through Dialogue of Spirituality

It has to be stated again that not all dialogue partners arrive at that high level of religious commitment that dialogue of spirituality requires. But some do reach it. If a believer through long-standing religious dedication has acquired deep convictions and internalized the practices of his or her religion, and if the person has succeeded in making a vital synthesis between religion and life, between belief and actual conduct, between creed and deeds, and between contemplation on eternal realities and involvement in active earthly engagements, then such a person is well placed to make dialogue of spirituality an important way of spiritual growth, or, as one would put it in Christian terms, a means to holiness.

Faithfully practiced, dialogue of spirituality will bring the person who engages in it nearer to God, through bringing the person nearer to other believers. The person can grow in humility, faith, praise, wisdom, and love. Such dialogue is not an activity irrelevant to religious or spiritual growth. It is very much a part of it.

Something wonderful happens when two deeply committed spiritual leaders of different religions meet. Because they are both sincerely and totally looking for God, they are able to understand each other better than two professors of their two religions who may speak the same language. Witnesses and lovers of God find that their hearts meet where perhaps the heads of the theologians and teachers have not met. Mystics and spiritually advanced people understand one another better and quicker than professors and theological technocrats. If believers who are charged with high voltages of spiritual energy continue to be active in interreligious contacts, they will grow further spiritually themselves. They will also be better placed to help their various religious communities to grow.

Conclusion: The Future of Dialogue

WHAT IS THE FUTURE OF INTERRELIGIOUS DIALOGUE? I AM NOT A prophet. I do not know. But this much I can say.

There are indeed obstacles on the road to dialogue. Apart from the usual difficulties, very disturbing are the rise of extremism and fundamentalism in some religions, the accompanying closing in on themselves by some believers in such religions, and the denial to others of the right to religious freedom in some parts of the world.

At the same time, the possibilities and potentialities of dialogue are many. And the results so far recorded are not inconsiderable. Think of the growth in mutual understanding and active collaboration unthinkable forty years ago. Consider the impact that interreligious dialogue has had on the Church, especially in her general approach to other believers, in her theology on salvation, and in her attention to the relationship between faith and culture. Take into account the effects of dialogue in other religions, especially in their willingness to open out to others. There has been a sharing of values in both directions. And there has been a greater appreciation of the role that cooperation between believers has to play if religion is to continue to be realistically present to a world that is thirsting for solidarity, development, high moral values, justice, peace, and love.

The balance is in favor of interreligious dialogue. Let it go on.